how to

MW00928530

Whether you're new to tarot, working with a new deck, or looking to deepen your connection, this journal offers ample space and useful prompts to help you on your tarot journey.

Each card has two dedicated pages for you to record your impressions and personal connections, the card's traditional meanings, and the symbols depicted in your deck, as well as space to sketch. Choose one card to study each day, or go at your own pace.

At the back you'll find two pages of sample questions and prompts to guide your readings, with space for your ideas. Use the following blank pages to sketch your favorite spreads and your ideas for new ones. Includes 30+ blank lined pages for notes and journaling.

SKETCHES/NOTES

the fool

SYMBOLS _____

_____

_____

_____

TRADITIONAL MEANINGS _____

_____

_____

_____

IMPRESSIONS _____

_____

_____

_____

_____

PERSONAL CONNECTIONS _____

_____

_____

_____

_____

SKETCHES/NOTES

the magician

SYMBOLS _____

_____

_____

_____

_____

TRADITIONAL MEANINGS _____

_____

_____

_____

_____

IMPRESSIONS _____

_____

_____

_____

_____

_____

PERSONAL CONNECTIONS _____

_____

_____

_____

_____

_____

SKETCHES/NOTES

the high priestess

SYMBOLS

TRADITIONAL MEANINGS

IMPRESSIONS

PERSONAL CONNECTIONS

SKETCHES/NOTES

the empress

SYMBOLS

TRADITIONAL MEANINGS

IMPRESSIONS

PERSONAL CONNECTIONS

SKETCHES/NOTES

the emperor

SYMBOLS

TRADITIONAL MEANINGS

IMPRESSIONS

PERSONAL CONNECTIONS

SKETCHES/NOTES

the hierophant

SYMBOLS _____

_____

_____

_____

TRADITIONAL MEANINGS _____

_____

_____

_____

_____

IMPRESSIONS _____

_____

_____

_____

_____

PERSONAL CONNECTIONS _____

_____

_____

_____

_____

SKETCHES/NOTES

the lovers

SYMBOLS

TRADITIONAL MEANINGS

IMPRESSIONS

PERSONAL CONNECTIONS

SKETCHES/NOTES

the chariot

SYMBOLS

TRADITIONAL MEANINGS

IMPRESSIONS

PERSONAL CONNECTIONS

SKETCHES/NOTES

SYMBOLS

TRADITIONAL MEANINGS

IMPRESSIONS

PERSONAL CONNECTIONS

SKETCHES/NOTES

the hermit

SYMBOLS _____

_____

_____

_____

TRADITIONAL MEANINGS _____

_____

_____

_____

IMPRESSIONS _____

_____

_____

_____

_____

PERSONAL CONNECTIONS _____

_____

_____

_____

_____

SKETCHES/NOTES

wheel of fortune

SYMBOLS

TRADITIONAL MEANINGS

IMPRESSIONS

PERSONAL CONNECTIONS

SKETCHES/NOTES

justice

SYMBOLS

TRADITIONAL MEANINGS

IMPRESSIONS

PERSONAL CONNECTIONS

SKETCHES/NOTES

the hanged man

SYMBOLS _____

_____

_____

_____

TRADITIONAL MEANINGS _____

_____

_____

_____

IMPRESSIONS _____

_____

_____

_____

PERSONAL CONNECTIONS _____

_____

_____

_____

_____

SKETCHES/NOTES

SYMBOLS

TRADITIONAL MEANINGS

IMPRESSIONS

PERSONAL CONNECTIONS

SKETCHES/NOTES

Temperance

SYMBOLS _____

_____

_____

_____

_____

TRADITIONAL MEANINGS _____

_____

_____

_____

_____

_____

IMPRESSIONS _____

_____

_____

_____

_____

_____

_____

PERSONAL CONNECTIONS _____

_____

_____

_____

_____

_____

SKETCHES/NOTES

the devil

SYMBOLS _____

_____

_____

_____

_____

TRADITIONAL MEANINGS _____

_____

_____

_____

_____

IMPRESSIONS _____

_____

_____

_____

_____

PERSONAL CONNECTIONS _____

_____

_____

_____

_____

_____

SKETCHES/NOTES

the tower

SYMBOLS

TRADITIONAL MEANINGS

IMPRESSIONS

PERSONAL CONNECTIONS

SKETCHES/NOTES

the star

SYMBOLS _____

_____

_____

_____

_____

TRADITIONAL MEANINGS _____

_____

_____

_____

_____

IMPRESSIONS _____

_____

_____

_____

_____

PERSONAL CONNECTIONS _____

_____

_____

_____

_____

SKETCHES/NOTES

the moon

SYMBOLS

TRADITIONAL MEANINGS

IMPRESSIONS

PERSONAL CONNECTIONS

SKETCHES/NOTES

the sun

SYMBOLS _____
_____
_____
_____

TRADITIONAL MEANINGS _____
_____
_____
_____
_____

IMPRESSIONS _____
_____
_____
_____
_____

PERSONAL CONNECTIONS _____
_____
_____
_____
_____

SKETCHES/NOTES

Judgement

SYMBOLS

TRADITIONAL MEANINGS

IMPRESSIONS

PERSONAL CONNECTIONS

SKETCHES/NOTES

the world

SYMBOLS

TRADITIONAL MEANINGS

IMPRESSIONS

PERSONAL CONNECTIONS

SKETCHES/NOTES

king of cups

SYMBOLS ♗K ~~Swan~~

TRADITIONAL MEANINGS Art. science. Creative.
water = Emotional Confident masculine
intuitive. master. certainty. Community

IMPRESSIONS ~~This is a difficult card to
read. Swan black stands alone
regal and wise. Removed.~~ Matured.

PERSONAL CONNECTIONS

SKETCHES/NOTES

queen of cups

SYMBOLS _____

_____

_____

_____

TRADITIONAL MEANINGS _____

_____

_____

_____

IMPRESSIONS _____

_____

_____

_____

_____

PERSONAL CONNECTIONS _____

_____

_____

_____

_____

SKETCHES/NOTES

knight of cups

SYMBOLS

TRADITIONAL MEANINGS

IMPRESSIONS

PERSONAL CONNECTIONS

SKETCHES/NOTES

page of cups

SYMBOLS

TRADITIONAL MEANINGS

IMPRESSIONS

PERSONAL CONNECTIONS

SKETCHES/NOTES

ten of cups

SYMBOLS

_____

_____

_____

_____

TRADITIONAL MEANINGS

_____

_____

_____

_____

IMPRESSIONS

_____

_____

_____

_____

PERSONAL CONNECTIONS

_____

_____

_____

_____

_____

SKETCHES/NOTES

nine of cups

SYMBOLS

TRADITIONAL MEANINGS

IMPRESSIONS

PERSONAL CONNECTIONS

SKETCHES/NOTES

eight of cups

SYMBOLS _____

_____

_____

_____

TRADITIONAL MEANINGS _____

_____

_____

_____

IMPRESSIONS _____

_____

_____

_____

_____

PERSONAL CONNECTIONS _____

_____

_____

_____

_____

SKETCHES/NOTES

seven of cups

SYMBOLS

TRADITIONAL MEANINGS

IMPRESSIONS

PERSONAL CONNECTIONS

SKETCHES/NOTES

six of cups

SYMBOLS

TRADITIONAL MEANINGS

IMPRESSIONS

PERSONAL CONNECTIONS

SKETCHES/NOTES

five of cups

SYMBOLS

TRADITIONAL MEANINGS

IMPRESSIONS

PERSONAL CONNECTIONS

SKETCHES/NOTES

four of cups

SYMBOLS

TRADITIONAL MEANINGS

IMPRESSIONS

PERSONAL CONNECTIONS

SKETCHES/NOTES

three of cups

SYMBOLS

TRADITIONAL MEANINGS

IMPRESSIONS

PERSONAL CONNECTIONS

SKETCHES/NOTES

two of cups

SYMBOLS _____

_____

_____

_____

TRADITIONAL MEANINGS _____

_____

_____

_____

IMPRESSIONS _____

_____

_____

_____

_____

PERSONAL CONNECTIONS _____

_____

_____

_____

_____

SKETCHES/NOTES

ace of cups

SYMBOLS _____

_____

_____

_____

TRADITIONAL MEANINGS _____

_____

_____

_____

IMPRESSIONS _____

_____

_____

_____

_____

PERSONAL CONNECTIONS _____

_____

_____

_____

_____

SKETCHES/NOTES

king of swords

SYMBOLS

TRADITIONAL MEANINGS

IMPRESSIONS

PERSONAL CONNECTIONS

SKETCHES/NOTES

queen of swords

SYMBOLS

TRADITIONAL MEANINGS

IMPRESSIONS

PERSONAL CONNECTIONS

SKETCHES/NOTES

knight of swords

SYMBOLS

TRADITIONAL MEANINGS

IMPRESSIONS

PERSONAL CONNECTIONS

SKETCHES/NOTES

page of swords

SYMBOLS

TRADITIONAL MEANINGS

IMPRESSIONS

PERSONAL CONNECTIONS

SKETCHES/NOTES

ten of swords

SYMBOLS

TRADITIONAL MEANINGS

IMPRESSIONS

PERSONAL CONNECTIONS

SKETCHES/NOTES

nine of swords

SYMBOLS

TRADITIONAL MEANINGS

IMPRESSIONS

PERSONAL CONNECTIONS

SKETCHES/NOTES

eight of swords

SYMBOLS

TRADITIONAL MEANINGS

IMPRESSIONS

PERSONAL CONNECTIONS

SKETCHES/NOTES

seven of swords

SYMBOLS

TRADITIONAL MEANINGS

IMPRESSIONS

PERSONAL CONNECTIONS

SKETCHES/NOTES

six of swords

SYMBOLS

TRADITIONAL MEANINGS

IMPRESSIONS

PERSONAL CONNECTIONS

SKETCHES/NOTES

five of swords

SYMBOLS

TRADITIONAL MEANINGS

IMPRESSIONS

PERSONAL CONNECTIONS

SKETCHES/NOTES

four of swords

SYMBOLS

TRADITIONAL MEANINGS

IMPRESSIONS

PERSONAL CONNECTIONS

SKETCHES/NOTES

three of swords

SYMBOLS

TRADITIONAL MEANINGS

IMPRESSIONS

PERSONAL CONNECTIONS

SKETCHES/NOTES

two of swords

SYMBOLS

TRADITIONAL MEANINGS

IMPRESSIONS

PERSONAL CONNECTIONS

SKETCHES/NOTES

ace of swords

SYMBOLS

TRADITIONAL MEANINGS

IMPRESSIONS

PERSONAL CONNECTIONS

SKETCHES/NOTES

king of wands

SYMBOLS

TRADITIONAL MEANINGS

IMPRESSIONS

PERSONAL CONNECTIONS

SKETCHES/NOTES

queen of wands

SYMBOLS

TRADITIONAL MEANINGS

IMPRESSIONS

PERSONAL CONNECTIONS

SKETCHES/NOTES

knight of wands

SYMBOLS

TRADITIONAL MEANINGS

IMPRESSIONS

PERSONAL CONNECTIONS

SKETCHES/NOTES

page of wands

SYMBOLS

_____

_____

_____

_____

TRADITIONAL MEANINGS

_____

_____

_____

_____

IMPRESSIONS

_____

_____

_____

_____

_____

PERSONAL CONNECTIONS

_____

_____

_____

_____

_____

SKETCHES/NOTES

ten of wands

SYMBOLS

TRADITIONAL MEANINGS

IMPRESSIONS

PERSONAL CONNECTIONS

SKETCHES/NOTES

nine of wands

SYMBOLS

TRADITIONAL MEANINGS

IMPRESSIONS

PERSONAL CONNECTIONS

SKETCHES/NOTES

eight of wands

SYMBOLS

TRADITIONAL MEANINGS

IMPRESSIONS

PERSONAL CONNECTIONS

SKETCHES/NOTES

seven of wands

SYMBOLS

TRADITIONAL MEANINGS

IMPRESSIONS

PERSONAL CONNECTIONS

SKETCHES/NOTES

six of wands

SYMBOLS

TRADITIONAL MEANINGS

IMPRESSIONS

PERSONAL CONNECTIONS

SKETCHES/NOTES

five of wands

SYMBOLS

TRADITIONAL MEANINGS

IMPRESSIONS

PERSONAL CONNECTIONS

SKETCHES/NOTES

four of wands

SYMBOLS

TRADITIONAL MEANINGS

IMPRESSIONS

PERSONAL CONNECTIONS

SKETCHES/NOTES

three of wands

SYMBOLS _____

_____

_____

_____

TRADITIONAL MEANINGS _____

_____

_____

_____

IMPRESSIONS _____

_____

_____

_____

_____

PERSONAL CONNECTIONS _____

_____

_____

_____

_____

SKETCHES/NOTES

two of wands

SYMBOLS

TRADITIONAL MEANINGS

IMPRESSIONS

PERSONAL CONNECTIONS

SKETCHES/NOTES

ace of wands

SYMBOLS _____

_____

_____

_____

TRADITIONAL MEANINGS _____

_____

_____

_____

IMPRESSIONS _____

_____

_____

_____

_____

PERSONAL CONNECTIONS _____

_____

_____

_____

SKETCHES/NOTES

king of pentacles

SYMBOLS _____
_____
_____
_____

TRADITIONAL MEANINGS _____
_____
_____
_____

IMPRESSIONS _____
_____
_____
_____

PERSONAL CONNECTIONS _____
_____
_____
_____
_____

SKETCHES/NOTES

queen of pentacles

SYMBOLS

TRADITIONAL MEANINGS

IMPRESSIONS

PERSONAL CONNECTIONS

SKETCHES/NOTES

knight of pentacles

SYMBOLS _____

_____

_____

_____

TRADITIONAL MEANINGS _____

_____

_____

_____

IMPRESSIONS _____

_____

_____

_____

_____

PERSONAL CONNECTIONS _____

_____

_____

_____

_____

SKETCHES/NOTES

page of pentacles

SYMBOLS _____

_____

_____

_____

_____

TRADITIONAL MEANINGS _____

_____

_____

_____

_____

IMPRESSIONS _____

_____

_____

_____

_____

_____

PERSONAL CONNECTIONS _____

_____

_____

_____

_____

_____

SKETCHES/NOTES

ten of pentacles

SYMBOLS

TRADITIONAL MEANINGS

IMPRESSIONS

PERSONAL CONNECTIONS

SKETCHES/NOTES

nine of pentacles

SYMBOLS

TRADITIONAL MEANINGS

IMPRESSIONS

PERSONAL CONNECTIONS

SKETCHES/NOTES

eight of pentacles

SYMBOLS

TRADITIONAL MEANINGS

IMPRESSIONS

PERSONAL CONNECTIONS

SKETCHES/NOTES

seven of pentacles

SYMBOLS _____

_____

_____

_____

TRADITIONAL MEANINGS _____

_____

_____

_____

_____

IMPRESSIONS _____

_____

_____

_____

_____

PERSONAL CONNECTIONS _____

_____

_____

_____

_____

_____

SKETCHES/NOTES

six of pentacles

SYMBOLS

TRADITIONAL MEANINGS

IMPRESSIONS

PERSONAL CONNECTIONS

SKETCHES/NOTES

five of pentacles

SYMBOLS _____

_____

_____

_____

TRADITIONAL MEANINGS _____

_____

_____

_____

_____

IMPRESSIONS _____

_____

_____

_____

_____

PERSONAL CONNECTIONS _____

_____

_____

_____

_____

SKETCHES/NOTES

four of pentacles

SYMBOLS _____

_____

_____

_____

TRADITIONAL MEANINGS _____

_____

_____

_____

_____

IMPRESSIONS _____

_____

_____

_____

_____

_____

PERSONAL CONNECTIONS _____

_____

_____

_____

_____

SKETCHES/NOTES

three of pentacles

SYMBOLS _____

_____

_____

_____

TRADITIONAL MEANINGS _____

_____

_____

_____

_____

IMPRESSIONS _____

_____

_____

_____

_____

PERSONAL CONNECTIONS _____

_____

_____

_____

_____

_____

SKETCHES/NOTES

two of pentacles

SYMBOLS _____

_____

_____

_____

TRADITIONAL MEANINGS _____

_____

_____

_____

IMPRESSIONS _____

_____

_____

_____

_____

PERSONAL CONNECTIONS _____

_____

_____

_____

_____

SKETCHES/NOTES

ace of pentacles

SYMBOLS

TRADITIONAL MEANINGS

IMPRESSIONS

PERSONAL CONNECTIONS

QUESTIONS & PROMPTS

WHAT MIGHT I EXPERIENCE IF...?

WHAT IS MY GREATEST STRENGTH?

HOW CAN I CREATE A LIFE OF WEALTH?

WHAT CAN I LEARN TODAY?

HOW AM I IN RELATIONSHIP TO...?

WHAT DO MY SPIRIT GUIDES WANT ME TO KNOW?

HOW CAN I SERVE OTHERS BEST?

WHAT IS IN ALIGNMENT WITH MY HIGHEST GOOD?

YOUR FAVORITE QUESTIONS & PROMPTS

QUESTIONS & PROMPTS

HOW CAN I BOOST MY ENERGY LEVELS?

WHAT SHOULD I FOCUS ON?

HOW CAN I MANIFEST MY DREAMS?

WHAT IS MY CALLING?

WHAT CAN I DO TO OVERCOME GRIEF?

HOW CAN I FULFILL MY POTENTIAL?

WHAT TALENTS AM I NOT UTILIZING?

HOW CAN I GROW AND EVOLVE?

YOUR FAVORITE QUESTIONS & PROMPTS

NEW & FAVORITE SPREADS

NEW & FAVORITE SPREADS

NEW & FAVORITE SPREADS

NEW & FAVORITE SPREADS

NEW & FAVORITE SPREADS

NOTES

NOTES

NOTES

NOTES

NOTES

NOTES

NOTES

NOTES

NOTES

NOTES

NOTES

NOTES

NOTES

NOTES

NOTES

NOTES

NOTES

NOTES

NOTES

NOTES

NOTES

NOTES

NOTES

NOTES

NOTES

NOTES

NOTES

NOTES

NOTES

NOTES

NOTES